SPOTLIGHT ON CIVIC ACTION

CIVIC ENGAGEMENT
HOW INDIVIDUALS AND INSTITUTIONS INTERACT

JOYCE MCCORMICK

PowerKiDS press™

NEW YORK

Published in 2018 by The Rosen Publishing Group, Inc.
29 East 21st Street, New York, NY 10010

Editor: Melissa Raé Shofner
Book Design: Michael Flynn
Interior Layout: Reann Nye

Photo Credits: Cover Hero Images/Getty Images; p. 4 https://commons.wikimedia.org/wiki/File:Alexis_de_tocqueville.jpg; p. 5 Rawpixel.com/Shutterstock.com; pp. 7, 20 wavebreakmedia/Shutterstock.com; p. 9 Courtesy of the Library of Congress; pp. 9, 13 (background) Evgeny Karandaev/Shutterstock.com; p. 11 Richard Nowitz/National Geographic/Getty Images; p. 13 https://commons.wikimedia.org/wiki/File:Constitution_of_the_United_States,_page_1.jpg; pp. 14, 15 Everett Historical/Shutterstock.com; p. 17 Robb Reece/Corbis Documentary/Getty Images; p. 18 Everett Collection/Shutterstock.com; p. 19 SpeedKingz/Shutterstock.com; p. 21 asiseeit/E+/Getty Images; p. 23 Image Source/Getty Images; p. 25 iJeab/Shutterstock.com; p. 26 Monkey Business Images/Shutterstock.com; p. 27 Diego G Diaz/Shutterstock.com; p. 29 Hill Street Studios/Eric Raptosh/Blend Images/Getty Images.

Cataloging-in-Publication Data

Names: McCormick, Joyce.
Title: Civic engagement: how individuals and institutions interact / Joyce McCormick.
Description: New York : PowerKids Press, 2018. | Series: Spotlight on civic action | Includes index.
Identifiers: ISBN 9781538327876 (pbk.) | ISBN 9781508163978 (library bound) | ISBN 9781538327999 (6 pack)
Subjects: LCSH: Social action--Juvenile literature. | Social advocacy--Juvenile literature. | Political participation--Juvenile literature.
Classification: HQ784.V64 M33 LCC 2018 | DDC 362.0425--dc23

Manufactured in China

CPSIA Compliance Information: Batch #BW18PK For further information contact Rosen Publishing, New York, New York at 1-800-237-9932.

CONTENTS

CHAPTER ONE

DEMOCRACY IN AMERICA

In the early 1830s, a Frenchman named Alexis de Tocqueville traveled to the United States for a research project. During his nine-month stay, he learned a lot about American society. Inspired by his observations, Tocqueville published the first part of his work *Democracy in America* in 1835. The second part was published in 1840.

Democracy in America explored Tocqueville's belief that the United States was an excellent example of how equality served democracy. Tocqueville used the term "individualism" to describe how American society emphasized the individual.

ALEXIS DE TOCQUEVILLE

A democracy is a type of government in which citizens actively **participate**, either directly or through representatives. "Democracy" comes from the Greek words *dēmos*, which means "people," and *kratia*, which means "power." In a democracy, the people have the power.

In his work, Tocqueville mentioned the dangers of an individualistic society, such as an unwillingness or inability to prevent **tyranny**. However, he also described how Americans overcame individualism by forming communities. Groups of people would come together when public reform was needed. This is known as civic engagement. It's what makes democracy work, even today.

CHAPTER TWO

WHAT IS CIVIC ENGAGEMENT?

Civic engagement may also be called civic responsibility, community involvement, or community participation. It's a broad term that refers to the act of people coming together to **enact** change that benefits their community, often by working with institutions such as schools and the U.S. government. The idea of civic engagement dates back more than 2,500 years to ancient Rome.

Communities are at the heart of civic engagement. A community may be a group of individuals who live or work in the same place. It may also be a group of individuals with common interests, ideas, or goals. The needs of a community drive civic participation.

Recall what Tocqueville said about individuals and communities in *Democracy in America*. To fully appreciate the role of civic engagement in the United States, it's important to first understand how the nation's government took shape.

Civic engagement brings people together to solve problems that affect their community. These groups of concerned citizens can enact change in common institutions, such as the U.S. government, universities, health-care facilities, and much more.

CHAPTER THREE

A YOUNG NATION

In 1776, about one year into the Revolutionary War, the Declaration of Independence was signed and the 13 American colonies declared themselves free of British rule. Together, the newly independent states were called the United States of America. It was an exciting time for the residents of the new country. However, even though the people of the United States claimed to be free and independent, the Revolutionary War continued.

The Americans knew they needed their own government to unite them. In 1781, the Articles of Confederation were **ratified** and became the first **constitution** of the United States. This constitution had many problems, though, and many people weren't happy with it. The new federal government was weak. Civic engagement was needed in order to make a change.

Here, Benjamin Franklin and Richard Oswald are seen discussing the Treaty of Paris, which formally ended the Revolutionary War in 1783. The British had surrendered in Yorktown, Virginia, two years earlier, but the fighting had continued.

CHAPTER FOUR

THE U.S. CONSTITUTION

In 1787, when the United States was still a very new country, a group of 55 men gathered in Philadelphia, Pennsylvania, to fix the Articles of Confederation. However, instead of fixing the old system, they ended up writing an entirely new system for their government— the U.S. Constitution.

The Constitution outlines the most basic laws of the United States and has served as the framework for the U.S. government for more than 200 years. The goal of the Constitution was to create a balanced and fair government that would be able to run the country without interfering with the rights of the states or individual citizens.

On March 4, 1789, the Constitution officially became the supreme law of the United States. To this day, all national, state, and local laws must follow this set of rules.

Today, you can view the U.S. Constitution at the National Archives in Washington, D.C. It's kept in a special case to protect it from the elements. It's displayed alongside the Declaration of Independence and the Bill of Rights.

CHAPTER FIVE

A REPRESENTATIVE DEMOCRACY

The Constitution divides power between three branches of government. The legislative branch makes laws, the judicial branch interprets laws, and the executive branch (which includes the president) carries out laws. A system of checks and balances is in place to keep any one branch from becoming too powerful.

The legislative branch, or Congress, is made up of the Senate and the House of Representatives. Members of these two bodies are elected by and serve as representatives of the American people. When Congress is creating new laws or making changes to existing laws, it's supposed to listen to what the people want. The representatives within the Senate and the House are able to voice the citizens' concerns and take action on their behalf. This makes the United States a representative democracy. It may also be considered a **republic**.

The Constitution begins with three important words: "We the people." The U.S. government is supposed to be a government of the people.

CHAPTER SIX

HAVING YOUR VOICE HEARD

Members of the House and the Senate serve as representatives for the people—but how do the people go about having their voices heard? The answer is civic engagement.

Civic engagement has helped bring about many great changes throughout the history of the United States. Remember when the American people were unhappy

Suffragists, or people fighting for the right to vote, rode horses through the streets of Washington, D.C., in 1914.

Civic engagement helped women in their fight for voting rights. In 1917, New York became one of the first states to allow women to vote. In 1920, the 19th Amendment was ratified, giving all American women the constitutional right to vote.

with the Articles of Confederation and a group of men came together to make a change? Through this act of civic engagement, the U.S. Constitution was created.

Today, registering to vote, participating in an election, or writing letters to your representatives are all great starting places for becoming more civically engaged. They're ways to let members of the Senate and the House, and ultimately all of Congress, know what matters to you and your community.

CHAPTER SEVEN

BEING AN ACTIVE CITIZEN

Civic engagement involves working toward change that is beneficial to you *and* your community. It works with our country's representative democracy and it often involves government institutions, but it doesn't have to be political. There are many ways to be an active and engaged citizen. Civic engagement gives people the power to create change in their communities on all levels.

There are many types of communities, and an individual may belong to a number of them at the same time. People often belong to more communities than they realize. A family is a type of community. Neighborhoods, towns, and cities are communities, too. Some people belong to organizations such as churches or clubs. These are all types of communities. Are you an active citizen in the communities to which you belong?

Some institutions, such as the Boy Scouts of America, are communities, too. So are colleges and your school and classroom.

Civic engagement happens all the time, even if you don't realize it. Simple, everyday acts of community participation such as reading a newspaper or talking to your neighbor are forms of civic engagement. Of course, you may take things a step further by talking to your neighbor about fixing an important local issue or helping another neighbor in need.

When someone sees an area of need within a community, they may use it as a point around which to gather. If a cause, such as the need to reduce homelessness or to start a trash cleanup effort, is important to one person, it may be important to others. These people can come together to work toward making a change. Talking to people in your community is the first step in making a difference.

CHAPTER EIGHT

OTHER WAYS TO MAKE A DIFFERENCE

Some forms of civic engagement are more obvious than others. Some take less time or less effort. One of the greatest things about civic engagement is that it comes in all shapes and sizes. If something matters to you, speak up about it and work toward making a change in your community. There's no right or wrong way to be an active citizen.

Volunteering for an organization such as Habitat for Humanity can make a big difference in a community. Habitat for Humanity has built more than 70,000 new homes for families in need since its founding in 1976. It's located in 1,400 communities across the United States.

Volunteering with an institution such as a government agency, public school, or nonprofit organization is civic engagement. You could also take action by becoming educated about an area of need and speaking to others about the issue. This is called advocacy. When you're civically engaged, it means you're taking actions that are informed, committed, and constructive. Understand an issue, stand behind the cause, and work toward positive change.

CHAPTER NINE

RECIPROCAL RELATIONSHIPS

Civic engagement can be driven by a need for change within a community. It's also driven by an individual's moral concern and sense of citizenship. It is, in large part, giving back to the community, but it also benefits the individual. There is a cycle of giving and receiving that occurs when someone is an active citizen. This pattern of giving to the community and receiving benefits in return can be described as a **reciprocal** relationship.

There are many things you can give that will benefit your community. Just a little of your time and energy can make a big difference. You may also be able to contribute money to a cause that's important to you. Sharing your knowledge about an issue can also be valuable.

In 2010, citizens in Albuquerque and Santa Fe, New Mexico, met with an organization called Everyday Democracy to discuss education issues. The New Mexico legislature enacted the Early Childhood Care and Education Act in part because of this civic engagement.

CHAPTER TEN

WHAT'S IN IT FOR YOU?

On the other side of the reciprocal relationship of civic engagement are countless benefits for individuals. By participating in a community, an individual can grow their social **network**, receive support from like-minded people, and gain a sense of belonging to a group. They may also gain a greater appreciation for community **diversity**.

Communities may offer a built-in support system that contributes to an individual's sense of self-worth and promotes higher self-esteem. Civically engaged people more often feel that problems can be overcome and goals can be achieved, thanks in part to the support they receive from their communities.

Civic engagement also provides individuals with important skills, such as planning, decision making, leadership, and communication. Active citizens have a greater sense of identity, direction, and purpose.

Tutoring can be a very rewarding form of civic engagement. You may be able to tutor a classmate, a younger student, or even an adult who is learning something new, such as how to speak English.

CHAPTER ELEVEN

TROUBLE CONNECTING

Being an active citizen may seem easy. There are opportunities to get involved all around us. Still, civic engagement presents problems for some people. Certain actions, such as signing **petitions** or donating money, don't keep citizens engaged on a consistent, or regular, basis. It's difficult for some people to see how small contributions such as these add up in the long run and make a difference.

Some people don't see marches and protests as effective pathways to change. However, these events bring together thousands and sometimes millions of people across the country. Gatherings of this size can definitely have an effect on public opinion and perhaps even lawmaking practices.

Some people view politicians in a negative light and feel many of them are only working for personal gain. This is another reason Americans should be civically engaged. Being informed about issues in their community allows individuals to form educated opinions and vote for representatives who share their views. Voting in local, state, and national elections is a way to have your voice heard on a greater level.

CHAPTER TWELVE

SERVICE LEARNING

To spark interest in civic engagement and jump-start involvement in local communities, some institutions offer service-learning opportunities. Service learning is a way for individuals to become directly involved with a cause. Through a combination of community service and civic education, service learning strengthens communities and teaches about civic engagement.

Colleges often offer service-learning opportunities. Some programs focus on the needs of local communities. Others, such as Learn and Serve America, offer students the opportunity to travel to places in need in other parts of the country and even other parts of the world. Service learning may be a requirement for certain areas of study. It may also be voluntary. In either case, it helps to raise awareness of and encourage an interest in civic engagement. Service learning allows young people to see firsthand how being an active citizen can create positive change.

After Hurricane Katrina destroyed much of the New Orleans area in August 2005, some students chose to spend their spring break providing aid to the area. Many schools organized service-learning trips to rebuild homes and help the community get back on its feet.

CHAPTER THIRTEEN

BE AN AGENT OF CHANGE

Civic engagement is an important part of American society. It gives the people power to enact change, which is the foundation of democracy. The reciprocal relationship between individuals, communities, and institutions provides benefits to all.

Being an active citizen is easy. A little time and effort can make a big difference, especially when there are many people working together. Opportunities are endless and civic engagement is all around us, all the time. Civic engagement allows people to enact change at all levels, locally and globally.

What directly affects you and your community? What do you care about? Take this opportunity to become an agent of change and have an **impact** on the issues you care about. Civic engagement is a way to have your voice heard.

GLOSSARY

constitution (kahn-stuh-TOO-shun) The basic laws by which a country, state, or group is governed.

diversity (duh-VUHR-suh-tee) The quality or state of having many different types, forms, or ideas.

donate (DOH-nayt) To give something in order to help a person or organization.

enact (ih-NAKT) To put something into action.

impact (IHM-pakt) A strong effect.

network (NET-wuhrk) A group of informally interconnected people.

participate (par-TIH-suh-payt) To take part in something.

petition (puh-TIH-shun) A formal written request to a leader or government regarding a particular cause.

ratify (RAA-tuh-fy) To formally approve.

reciprocal (rih-SIH-pruh-kuhl) Shared, felt, or shown by both sides.

republic (rih-PUH-blik) A country governed by elected representatives and an elected leader.

tutor (TOO-tuhr) To provide someone with private instruction.

tyranny (TEER-uh-nee) Unfair treatment by people with power over others.

INDEX

PRIMARY SOURCE LIST

Page 4
Portrait of Alexis de Tocqueville. Oil painting. Théodore Cassériau. 1850. Now kept at the Palace of Versailles, France.

Page 13
First page of the U.S. Constitution. 1787. Now kept at the National Archives and Records Administration, Washington, D.C.

Page 15
Female suffragists casting votes in New York City. Photograph. 1917. From Shutterstock.com.

Page 27
Women's March in Portland, Oregon. Photograph. Diego G. Diaz. January 21, 2017. From Getty Images.

WEBSITES

Due to the changing nature of Internet links, PowerKids Press has developed an online list of websites related to the subject of this book. This site is updated regularly. Please use this link to access the list: www.powerkidslinks.com/sociv/civen